VISUAL INSPECTION[1]

VISUAL INSPECTION

MATT RADER

a blewointment book

NIGHTWOOD EDITIONS

2019

Nightwood Editions
P.O. Box 1779, Gibsons, BC, VON 1VO, Canada
www.nightwoodeditions.com

EDITOR: Amber McMillan
COVER ART: Katie Brennan
COVER DESIGN & TYPOGRAPHY: Carleton Wilson

Canada

Canada Council   Conseil des Arts
for the Arts   du Canada

BRITISH COLUMBIA
ARTS COUNCIL
An agency of the Province of British Columbia

Nightwood Editions acknowledges the support of the Canada Council for the Arts, which last year invested $153 million to bring the arts to Canadians throughout the country. Nous remercions le Conseil des arts du Canada de son soutien. L'an dernier, le Conseil a investi 153 millions de dollars pour mettre de l'art dans la vie des Canadiennes et des Canadiens de tout le pays. We also gratefully acknowledge financial support from the Government of Canada and from the Province of British Columbia through the BC Arts Council and the Book Publishing Tax Credit.

This book has been produced on 100% post-consumer recycled, ancient-forest-free paper, processed chlorine-free and printed with vegetable-based dyes.

Printed and bound in Canada.

LIBRARY AND ARCHIVES CANADA CATALOGUING IN PUBLICATION

Title: Visual inspection / Matt Rader.

Names: Rader, Matt, 1978- author.

Identifiers: Canadiana (print) 20189047968 | Canadiana (ebook) 20189047976
| ISBN 9780889713567

(softcover) | ISBN 9780889711440 (ebook)

Classification: LCC PS8585.A2825 V57 2019 | DDC C818/.6—dc23

for Elisa, who got me looking

&

for Jordan and Carmen, who showed me the way

TABLE OF CONTENTS

if you'll let a guide direct you
who only has at heart your getting lost

– Robert Frost

I respectfully acknowledge the syilx / ʔuknáqin people on whose traditional and unceded territory we conducted this research and art-making.

Introduction

I was born with difficulty breathing. Doctors guessed cystic fibrosis. They were wrong. My first memory is of being in hospital. Several internal organs were enlarged; they were testing for cancer. Rows of cribs. Large hands. Wires and machines. I was less than a year old. I did not have cancer. My mother carried me, blue and gasping, into the Emergency Room more times than she can recollect over those first three years. At four, when we moved from the city to a small fishing village on Vancouver Island, my mum insisted on a house within minutes of the hospital. 1980s. We'd go to the hospital in the evening. They'd shoot me with adrenaline. After, in the late hours of the night (it is always night in my memory), my eyes wide, my heart racing, I'd dash through the house, careening off the wainscotting in the basement, jumping from the back of the good couch, collecting myself from the carpet, from the linoleum, full of the drug our bodies produce when we most fear for our lives. I don't remember fearing for my life. I imagine the nurses and doctors feared for my life. In saving my life, they injected that fear into my body. Literally.

I know my mother feared for my life. She spent the first eighteen years helping me seek an answer. We searched daily. We accepted some stories. We rejected others. Nothing explained what happened with me beyond the idea of hyperactive immune responses to my environment. To my emotions. All treatments addressed symptoms, nothing else.

When I took over the search in my twenties, my largely inexplicable medical history continued to accumulate—I had the rarest form of appendicitis the weekend my mum moved from my childhood home after her divorce; I saw five specialists to address why half my lip had been swollen for a year (Guess what the answer was? No answer); and I did trials of breathing medications for three years, measuring the "peak flow" of my breath four times a day, every day. By the time I was thirty I was wracked by pervasive and debilitating pain.

Sometimes searching for something guarantees you'll never find it. Sometimes what you are looking for obscures what it is you find in your search; you have to see not what you're looking for but what is there.

Pain is different from suffering. Pain is a condition of the physical body. It can be assuaged, or it can't. To suffer is to insist, emotionally, that things be different, to refuse clarity. "Be whole beyond confusion," Robert Frost writes in "Directive," the poem from which I've borrowed the epigraph to this book. In that poem, to return to a place that no longer exists, and to become whole again, can only be achieved by getting lost. Though many people in pain suffer, this is the basic difference between pain and suffering: clarity or confusion. To be sure, clarity can, often does, increase pain; but it relieves suffering.

I've rarely suffered from my health. I've even more rarely written about it explicitly. My health, in all its qualities, good and poor, is a basic fact of my life and indistinguishable from my existence. Where do you locate health in your body? Easier to ask where you locate poor health? Curious that only certain qualities of health seem to assert themselves on the conscious level. In my writing—in my poems specifically—I've always felt my health—my body—as a silent, invisible, but active presence; it is there because the materials of the poems—the language—are sifted through my body. I didn't know how to make it explicit and I didn't feel a need to.

Robert Pinsky writes, in *The Sounds of Poetry*, that the instrument of the poet is the breath of the reader. And if the poet is the first reader, as Paul Muldoon asserts in *The End of the Poem*, the poet's breath is the instrument of composition. If you listen, you can hear Charles Olson in the hazy Blue Ridge Mountains sighing wearily, *I told you so.*

The world is experienced through our bodies. Our ideas are formed less than we'd like to admit through intellect; we have feelings (or experiences, as T.S. Eliot would have it) and through them we arrive at what we say we know.

From 2015–2017, I conducted a research-creation project at the University of British Columbia Okanagan called Visual Inspection. "Research-creation" is the term the Canadian academy uses to describe academic research projects with artistic outcomes. Though dressed up as academic inquiry, Visual Inspection was always, first and foremost, an art project conducted by artists.

Originally, the project asked a basic question: If the page is a field of visual composition in contemporary poetry—and it *is* such a field—how can we as poets make this field available to non-visual learners in a manner that is consistent with our own individual aesthetic preferences? What would we make?[2]

At first this seemed like a translation problem: How to account for the white space and typographic experiments in a poetic composition through audio or haptic renditions? Think recordings of poems read aloud, braille, or even poems printed in 3D according to a particular algorithm. With this wrinkle: How to also appeal to the poet as a poet, to be consistent with the poet's compositional practice, with the pleasure and realization of that practice?

It was important that this was a compositional question rather than a critical one. It was not praxis even but something more instinctual, something approaching from the opposite direction having yet to encounter the need for a term like "praxis." It was important because the site of inquiry existed beyond the scope of critical assessment as such in the realm of beauty, art and the good.[3]

But soon, even more a priori concerns appeared.

It is axiomatic, but worth stating nonetheless, that our lives are shaped by our bodies, how our bodies function, how they interact with our environments, both social and ecological. And if our bodies shape our lives then they must also shape our poems.

When I began the project in the fall of 2014, I was having considerable difficulty typing as the result of several immunological conditions, some that had been with me from the start, and others that had developed in adulthood. At times, I couldn't even hold open a book.

Over the course of the project my life was dramatically shaped by these conditions. Among other things I made upwards of three hundred visits to the Rutland Aurora Health Clinic, a space dedicated to people with complicated health histories and/or precarious socioeconomic statuses. I received more than six hundred injections. I travelled throughout British Columbia to see specialists in rheumatology, immunology, respirology, internal medicine, dermatology and psychiatry. Both at home and away, I received massage therapy, Trager massage, physiotherapy, chiropractic treatments, acupuncture, hypnosis, cupping, moxibustion, chakra healing, Qigong and traditional Chinese medicine. Twice I received emergency, life-saving medical intervention. I spent four days trussed to an IV on a hospital bed across from a room called "Dirty Service" in the hallway of 4B at Kelowna General Hospital. For two years, I spent sixty to seventy minutes of my day, every day, attached to a machine that helped me breathe. Never mind the details of my austere diet and the regime of pharmaceuticals I experimented with. Never mind the hundreds of hours travelling for treatment or given up to convalescences.

How did this shape my poetry? The list above is a chain of references awash in connotation: it employs specific elements of my life to suggest something more general about what it was like in this body over the years of the Visual Inspection project. This book is a similarly devised response to the question of how bodies shape poetry.[4]

Under the Hampton New Scholars Award, the primary grant funding Visual Inspection, I named two formal collaborators: poet Jordan Scott and social practice artist Carmen Papalia. Both Scott, who has a significant stutter, and Papalia, who is legally blind, had, through close attention, used their bodies as sites of artistic composition.[5]

In one such composition, Scott designed poems to challenge his ability to say them out loud, thus creating a collaboration between the text and his body in which his body became a vehicle for endless variations of the poems.[6] In one of Papalia's works, he has a small marching band follow him through a city street playing directional cues as he performs everyday tasks like buying a burrito.

And this too is axiomatic but bears repeating nonetheless: There is no body from which all other bodies might be assessed for deviation. Only the body of our imaginations, of culture. Similarly, there is no normal poetry, syntax, grammar or typography. There are only the normative categories cultures practice at any given moment in history.

A while ago, Papalia stopped using the word "blind" to describe himself and replaced it with "non-visual learner," because there is also no normal blind body, only many iterations of bodies with differing relationships to sight and visual information.

The narrative frame of the text that composes most of this book is an "eyes-closed" walking tour Papalia led for about thirty-five people in July of 2016 through a portion of downtown Kelowna. Just as that tour stretched and accordioned, stumbled and stalled and continued, as people called out obstacles down the line and slapped railings so we could hear what was coming, as the presence and commentary of passersby became important aspects of the tour experience, this text proceeds in fragments, associations and leaps, dragging in a number of histories, references and preoccupations. Like the tour, it is possible, likely even, that it arrives where it began. Like the tour, this may even be by design, though that is probably revisionist history.

As I write elsewhere, in the end, perhaps the best I can say about the questions raised by this project is that I've had thoughts. This is a record of some of those thoughts.

Notes

I hear the tangy slap of skin on metal as all the hands in front of me
pass along the railing. My right hand waves at the air.

Nothing.

                              Nothing.

Then:
                    the railing,

round and cold, with what feels like an uneven paint job,

as though parts of what had covered the metal had

been picked away,

                                        flaked off, so that
my fingers run across small ridges, tiny lips

              marking the border between one layer[7]

              of façade and the next.

We begin in an empty courtyard in the middle of what is called, on city signage, "the cultural district," a Richard Florida-inspired project occupying roughly three-by-three blocks of the northwest section of downtown.

We are thirty-five people, each with an arm or two touching the person in front of us—

touch is never pure or innocent—[8]

our eyes closed, following a man named Carmen, a man with a cane who doesn't see, through a city he visited for the first time two days earlier.

I'm near

the end

of the line.

To follow is to be guided.

When I was a boy, I knew a man who'd been a big-game guide in the Yukon until his cabin at Burwash Landing burned down and he came to live with us in our fishing village on the Salish Sea.

Dante's famous guide to the underworld was the Roman poet Virgil, whose family had been displaced from their land in the shift from the Republic to the Empire.

In Book VI of Virgil's *Aeneid*, a pair of doves[9] guides Aeneas to the Golden Bough. Aeneas must return the bough to a sibyl from the Temple of Apollo.

In exchange, she guides him to the Gates of Dis, as has been prophesized.

Walking, we map a space in time. What exists in that space.

Many people have written about walking. Many more about existence.[10] Will the real Martin Heidegger please stand up?

From Inger Christensen's book-length fib,[11] *Alphabet*:

cicadas exist; chicory, chromium / citrus trees; cicadas exist;
/ cicadas, cedars, cypresses, the cere-bellum // doves exist,
dreamers, and dolls; killers exist, and doves, and doves; haze,
dioxin, and days; days / exist, days and death; and poems / exist;
poems, days, death

From the lake moving east and north,

the cultural district includes an outdoor skating rink,

a yacht club,

a Cactus Club,

a brewery,

a Delta Grand Hotel and Casino

where a famous mobster was gunned down

while climbing into a white Porsche SUV

on August 4, 2011—

The Grand is sinking, our docent quips. We're standing in the central room at the Sncəwips Heritage Museum, between her cousin's mx̌ʷal / cradle board and the čʼaɫqʷm̓ display the docent uses to play this traditional gambling game with us. My friend and I keep winning.[12]

Then we guide our minds—the docent, her supervisor, my friend and I—to another time without concrete. Her colleague tells us what he sees: wetlands, tule, creeks completely full with dappled salmon, people.

A path has no beginning or end but in the direction you take it. *You don't have to follow an animal if you know where it is going,* her colleague says. *Only wait in the right place for it to arrive.*

One August when I was nine years old, crossing from Experiment Bight to Nels Bight on the northern-most coast of Vancouver Island, our man from Burwash Landing spotted wolf tracks in the sand. He guided us, crouched and then on our bellies, to the lip of the dune from where we could see a she-wolf leading three pups at a trot down the beach.

—a community theatre called / The Community Theatre, a
blackbox // theatre called / The Blackbox, Provincial law / courts,
the city art gallery, // the city museum, a military / museum,
an old indoor / hockey rink called Memorial / Arena, the main
RCMP // detachment and city jail, / the downtown branch of / the
Regional Library, the city / Mental Health and Substance Use //
Clinic, The Wine and Fruit / Museum and The Rotary Centre / for
the Arts which includes // an artist run / gallery, a theatre, dance
/ studios, arts admin offices, / a handful of artist / studios and a
coffee // shop—

I've thought of those wolves so often I've not been able to write them down.

Until now.

"A story is a simple thing," my friend Moshe once told me. "Just tell it."

Tule. Dappled salmon. Merlin. Can you see them? In this phase, they are hidden like the new moon. Like a thimblerig. A card trick. The c̓aÌ́q̌ʷm̓ sticks behind the back. Which hand?[13]

"Increasingly," writes Karen Barad, "I find myself drawn to poetics as a mode of expression."[14]

—a youth theatre / space in one alley, a couple // of private galleries, a shuttered night- /club, and a mid-sized // hockey arena named after / a credit // union with a restaurant / called after // a borough of New York City / and a VIP lounge // sponsored by a Canada- /wide realty company—[15]

Traffic exists. Slow traffic. Slowness exists; and sidewalks, bikes exist, bikes and traffic; pedestrians, sidewalks, shopping bags exist; slowness, sidewalks, traffic—

I've never heard a resident of this city use the term "cultural district" without sarcasm.

Mostly, we don't use the term at all.[16]

In the summer, the city wheels out a few upright pianos for people to plunk out wobbly melodies. Someone is playing "Karma Police" as we depart.

Several large concrete representations of fruit line the pedestrian alley between the Rotary Centre and the Blackbox.

On the nearby hills, the semi-arid shrub-steppe carries on its gathering of sagebrush and grasses.[17]

br

e

/   a

k

When I close my eyes in the courtyard between the Rotary Centre and the city art gallery, the sky is a dull solution of silver bromide. As I walk with my eyes closed, the day appears to brighten and brighten through my eyelids.

What we see as light and colour is the expression of several relationships: photons from the sun with the reflective surfaces of our environments, with the rods and cones of our eyes, with the neuropathways in our brain.

I read about these relationships in a book on the discoveries of cognitive science and their implications for philosophical traditions.

The book was written by a famous cognitive scientist from the United States and a philosopher with whom I once spoke when I was in graduate school ten years earlier. We were standing before our respective urinals, legs braced in that way that betrays a particular concentration. I mentioned John Dewey's aesthetic theory. He nodded.

Another word for this kind of phenomenon is coincidence. From coincidence might come something new: colour for example, or this anecdote. Brought together, the elements do what? Collaborate?

At first my hand is on the shoulder of a young Iranian-Canadian sculptor with a rare blood disorder. He's several inches taller than me, 6'2" maybe, thin but broad shouldered.

Recently, he'd installed a series of geometric shapes on my living room wall. The shapes are made of translucent, pastel-coloured bendy straws and translucent scotch tape. Affixed with Velcro, the straws appear to be growing like crystals from the white paint and drywall.

While he mounted the sculpture, we talked about the maintenance of his blood and the limitations it put on travel, how his blood is always a factor.

As we walk he drinks coffee with one hand, eyes closed, his other hand on my shoulder.[18]

By 1654, John Milton was completely blind. He titled his most famous poem of that period, "When I Consider How My Light is Spent"—a delightfully multivalent phrase that turns on both the light that vision afforded him and its diminishment, as well as the metaphor of his life and life's work being kinds of light.

A later editor retitled the sonnet, "On His Blindness."

By 1977, Ronald Johnson had completed a deep erasure of Milton's masterpiece, *Paradise Lost*, which he published as *Radi os*.

The term "radio" comes from the combining form of the Latin noun "radius," meaning ray or beam. Such as a ray of light. A sunbeam.

There's this thing I like to do. Just to get a sense of who is here. We close our eyes and then we say our names. I say my name and then you each say your name. If you think you're the last person you're probably not. We'll get through this quickly.

I'm closing my eyes, I promise.

My eyes are closed.

Ronald Johnson's book of erasure poetry—in which new poems are discovered[19] in existing texts by cutting away most of the original text—has four customer reviews on Amazon and a 100 percent, five-star rating.

A cookbook, *The American Table*, also attributed to Ronald Johnson, is a collaboration with illustrator James McGarrell; it has ten customer reviews and an identical 100 percent, five-star rating.[20]

As if in anticipation of this confluence of poetry and meals, the final line of "When I Consider How My Light is Spent" reads, "they also serve who only stand and wait."

b / r

/ k

Some people like to be read to and other people do not.

Until the age of six my eldest daughter enjoyed hearing novels read aloud. Then she didn't like novels at all. Then, at the age of ten, she started reading them to herself, silently, in her head.

I heard somewhere that Jorge Luis Borges, whose progressive blindness reached maturation at age fifty-five, thirty years before his death, had a rotating crew of young people who read to him at the library in his mother's home in Buenos Aires.

Some critics feel that Borges's blindness prompted him to develop intricate, imaginative worlds.

Such is the double bind of the mythologized blind: unseeing and all-seeing at once.

If my daughter reads silently in her head, then where does Borges read in the voices of young readers?

In a guided meditation, I'm invited to close my eyes.

After a series of descending numbers and images, I'm relaxed and I visit an island.

I look around.

The island is russet-coloured and black. A couple dozen metres in diameter. Barren. Large white seabirds glide down from the milk-blue sky, perch on the rock, then flap away. I'm standing on a beach of fine round pebbles the ocean combs through as it recedes.

Downpour, sluice-rush, spillage and backwash/ Come flowing through… / You stand there like a pipe / Being played by water… / And diminuendo runs through all its scales… [21]

This is what I know: the island is still warm. As if it were new. As if in this place, deep inside myself, human time and geological time are unified.

After about thirty minutes of shuffling along with our eyes closed,
kicking the heels of the person in front of us, apologizing, trying to
find the rhythm, the pace, the Iranian-Canadian sculptor steps out
of the line to pee, carefully taking my hand from his shoulder

and giving it to the person in front of him, one of the guest artists
visiting for the week, someone I'd met several summers before on
another island in the Salish Sea,

someone who, like me, lives with chronic, uncontrollable pain.[22]

Pain either obliterates the world or becomes the world. Elaine Scarry says something like this in her book *The Body in Pain*.

Think stubbing your toe. The world collapses into the absolute gravity of the acute injury from which no light escapes—

or it radiates until every contact hurts, until everything is the searing light of pain. *Paradise Lost. Radi os.*

An old man, talking of his controversial work with Haida myth and story, once said that sometimes one's injuries are so great that to simply be regarded hurts.

The old man may be wrong about the Haida but right about pain.

Reaching back, Taryn takes my hand and guides it to her shoulder. *Is this okay?* I ask.

She is several inches shorter than me. I think of my voice, my breath, coming from just above and behind her.

Touch is never innocent. Touch is never innocent?

Throughout my life, when I've been sick and quiet, I've heard two voices, one male and one female, calling my name from a distance behind me and slightly above.

Yes, she says, then a few minutes later she asks me to place my hand lower on her arm.

Through the clear window

of the cornea, light

          bends and opens

      in the iris. "At the end of my suffering,"
        says the wild iris

in Glück's poem, "there was a door." At the back of my eye
the convergence

      comes into focus. This is how

        the eye works.

How does it feel to blackout, to erase, the poems of a blind man?

We are climbing the steps of the law courts in single file, slowly, the head of the line calling back warnings: *Post! Gate! Post!*

In 2017, six years after the shooting of the gangster in the Porsche suv that also left a young woman paralyzed, the trial of his alleged murderers begins in this courthouse. There are cameras everywhere and security detail with guns.

My hand runs along the railing. What is solid, classical physics tells us, is solid because of electromagnetic repulsion: the inability of subatomic particles to bear touch.

Justice, in all the statues, is blind.[23]

b /

re /

a / k

A few days before our walk, Jordan gives a talk at the Alternator Centre for Contemporary Art, the artist-run gallery within the Rotary Centre where our walk begins.

His talk that Friday night in July is, in part, about what he could write with one hand while holding his baby—

Children make everything both infinitely complicated and utterly simple,

I have said a hundred times—

and, in part, about a week he spent documenting disfluency, absence and non-visual space at the Guantanamo Bay detention camp in Guantánamo Bay, Cuba.[24]

When I encounter an obstacle, I will call it out and every third person will pass the call down the line.

Let's practice.

Water.

Water.

Water.

Water.

Water.

Water.

Water.

Water.

Water.

Water.

Good.

If the line breaks, call BREAK! *and we will all stop until the line reattaches itself.*[25]

Jordan's thought about disfluency for a long time.

The stammer as mendacity. Moses with the burning coal in his mouth.

In an earlier work, Jordan teamed up with a colleague to place copies of Darwin's *On the Origin of Species* in different bioregions of British Columbia,

giving the biochemical forces of those regions a year to perform their own disfluent erasure poems on one of the visionary texts of contemporary scientific thought.

What's true, research suggests, is that the more fluent your story, the more likely it is to be false.[26]

The line a c c o r d i o n s   then

snaps.

We're in traffic,
                    the middle of the road,
        cars braked

                        and humming a few feet away.
                        Someone,

a few positions ahead, has lost touch[27]

        with the person who guides them.

            BREAK   *BREAK*

With our eyes closed we feel exposed, open
        to the touch of a gaze

                our own gaze

cannot deflect. Who trusts the drivers

                to see us? And not

            to see us?[28]

To be sensitive is to perceive finely. A sensitive instrument.

To be sensitive is to overreact.

One description of electrons is as particles at the edge of a mostly empty atom, hypersensitive to touch.

What are they doing, Mama?

I don't know.

I think they're learning to walk.

Denise. Erin. Karolina. Ashok. Ruth. David. Carol. Shelby. Lily. Erin. Michael. ███████ *Katherine. Rodrigo.* ████████ *Pat. Emily. Omar. Rebecca. Emma. Ollie.* ███ *Tomas.* ██ *Tanis.* ████████ ████████ *Taryn. Dara. Matt. Clay. Carmen.*[29]

As Jordan reports it, poetry by detainees at the Guantanamo Bay detention camp is routinely redacted in its entirety.

Power knows that poetry, performed well, trades in the multiple, the multivalent, the ineffable but deeply felt excess of experience. Such poetry is, by composition, an alternative to any hegemonic force because it imagines two simultaneous coordinates of meaning:

the semantic and the extra-semantic.[30]

Before the man from Burwash Landing lived with us, he renounced most possessions.

He wasn't from Burwash Landing even, though that is how he is known in this story.

Things he kept: a spotting scope powerful enough to see the ridges of the moon, a planisphere that could be turned to reveal seasonal maps of the night sky, a bear skull he kept wrapped in newspaper in a cardboard box below his bed.

A bear's skull, he showed me, looks like a human's only larger; it holds attention and returns it.

Power feeds on the singular, the containable, the reducible. Power cannot trust poetry. Power knows that poetry, for all its popular disdain and inscrutability, can contain messages—codes—Power is blind and deaf to.

Poetry can, in this sense, disable Power.

Therefore, in transcripts and other documents pertaining to detainees at Guantanamo Bay, poems appear as carefully blacked-out lines from margin to margin. In these pages, even the white space is redacted.[31]

What pain. What brutality.

"In the remarkable poem 'The Snow Man,'" writes Robert Pack,
"Wallace Stevens dramatizes the action of a mind as it becomes one
with the scene it perceives,

and at that instant, the mind having ceased to bring something of
itself to the scene, the scene then ceases to exist fully."

To *my* mind, this is the kind of bullshit Power abhors.

32

Walking with my eyes closed, my hand on Taryn's shoulder, I smell cut grass and lake water.

All my life I've been allergic to cut grass.[33]

Then I hear footsteps on metal.

        The line snakes to the right one step then

back to the left.

I guess we're crossing the locks behind the Delta Grand where the lake used to be,

and a ferry landing. Sawmill waste. Clay. Silt. Sand. Lacustrine deposits. Now ten meters of soil and a concrete raft slab.

For more than a hundred years, this shore-

        line has been redacted.

b

a

ɘ

r

/

On Pincushion Mountain one morning, the saskatoons airing
their white-linen bloom along the trail, the garland of kinnikinnick
vining the rocky summit, I remain a poet caught up in language and
images.

Across the canyon to the north, four turkey vultures roost.

Then, one by one, they cross the canyon and make wide circling
passes close enough that I can see their wattle-coloured heads.

Some new thinkers—philosophers, physicists, tech gurus, futurists—say that what we see of the world is only "the desktop," the representation of a much more complex "reality" in a form that our embodied selves can manipulate.[34] In this they resemble all the old thinkers.[35]

This table is not solid, classical physics tells us, because it is made of subatomic particles that are themselves mostly empty space. That space is redacted by our mass in relationship to the mass of the table.

Even less solid: our own body, composed as we are of so many organisms that are not strictly "human," according to current taxonomies of Power.[36]

I dig my fingers into Taryn's back but don't notice until she tells me to stop.

To one side now would be a large grassy berm that is one part of an outdoor amphitheatre, to the other a series of canals that connect the hotel and casino complex to a complex of apartment towers called the Waterscapes, known for the large fountain out front that depicts three white, frolicking dolphins in a city four hundred kilometres from the ocean. The fountain sculpture is titled "Euphoria."

A voice rises ahead of me and a phrase travels back, call by call, to those of us at the tail end of the line, a phrase

I repeat for the benefit of no one: *Water to your right.*

To have an allergy is to be hypersensitive. When a mower kicks pollen from the grasses into the air, immunoglobulin E antibodies in my immune system bind to the pollens and then to a receptor on mast cells triggering the release of histamine, an inflammatory chemical meant to help the body flush toxins.

The feeling of entering a space full of allergens might be analogous to the aura some people experience before a migraine, or the smell (popularly of burnt toast) reported by epileptics just prior to a seizure.

The tissues in my eyes and nostrils begin to swell. In some cases, food tastes rotten and everything stinks of smoke.

Then my chest tightens.

On Pincushion, the slow vortex of vultures guides me back to earlier vultures circling a blown-out tire on Interstate 5 somewhere north of Eugene, Oregon.

For a moment, the memory of vultures and the vultures overhead that day are simultaneous, almost as they appear on this page.

Then the vortex is a kitchen drain draining presence and corporeal apprehension into memory so that the sky is, briefly, of another, earlier time.

Later, I will think of the vultures as hags, witches turning the cauldron of the sky. And then as the shades of the dead summoned by Odysseus with milk and the blood of a black ewe.

k

/

/

a

The story of the immune system in Western medicine is a story of war, identity and perception. In the West, the immune system identifies, attacks, isolates and either destroys or excretes foreign pathogens and poisons.

Immunological disorders largely fall into two camps: utter failure to mount a defense, usually due to a structural problem such as too few white blood cells, or utter misapprehension of harmless, or even beneficial, substances (allergens) including the body itself (autoimmune disease).

What story to tell you, the acupuncturist murmurs, when I ask a question about pain in my hands.

What stories to tell about the Walking Tour? About redaction? About my body?

The story, though, is only part of the story.

When I talk you through relaxation and visualization, the acupuncturist says matter-of-factly, *my voice replaces your inner voice, and the mind of the body can take over.*

Minds are collaborative spaces. As are bodies.

At thirty I began to experience persistent, debilitating pain in my shoulders, hands and hips.

I'd jog for an hour, as I had for years, then come home and collapse on my bed and cry. I couldn't type.

I couldn't hold open a book.

Blood tests showed no elevation in acute-phase inflammatory markers. No reactive protein (CRP) rise. No spike in the erythrocyte sedimentation rate (ESR).[37]

Then the pain began to manifest throughout my body.

Voices further up the line conspire about their day as though they might be anywhere doing anything.

How to describe the waves of movement sent forward and backward through our arms and shoulders? My mind deep in meta-narrative, registering sensation immediately as a compositional problem.

Part of my body goes forward, then another part backward. I can't stand up straight and my back hurts.

I've learned not to pay too close attention to the tightening in my chest. If I keep singing I will not stutter.

Behind me I hear chatter, shuffles. Someone joins. I turn my head back out of instinct, but my eyes are closed. I remember to keep my eyes closed.

If only Orpheus had walked with his eyes closed.

That's a mythological theme: regret, shame, memory, the past. The irony of looking as ruination. Just ask Medusa, Narcissus.

"Oh hello, my shadow," I wrote in a poem. "Hello, regret."

But why did he look back? A failing of faith that Eurydice was right behind? A failing of trust? Fear of being made a fool?

Dont Look Back, D.A. Pennbaker's 1967 Bob Dylan documentary got its name from Satchel Paige who reportedly said, "Don't look back. Something might be gaining on you."

To suffer is to look toward a time and place beyond one's suffering, to fear that such a destination will never be reached.

Don't worry, we might say. *Fear is always fear of something yet to happen.*

When we see a printed haiku by Bashō we immediately, before reading a word, apprehend something different than when we see the first page of a blank-verse epic like *Paradise Lost*.

38

39

We have different expectations of, and relationships with, these texts, even before we begin to decode them semantically—expectations and relationships that can't help but influence a reader's attitude toward them.

How then, as composers, to account for these virtually instantaneous impressions in sound or touch?

How to create versions of our poems, or even compose poems, that render these extra-semantic dimensions available to the non-visual learner?[40]

"Rendition," according to Wikipedia, is the practice of sending a "foreign combatant" to a territory with "less rigorous regulations for the humane treatment of prisoners." It is also the term for processing animal flesh into food.

k

e

/

a

—

▬

Jordan Scott's *Clearance Process*, the digital, multimedia chapbook that recounts his week in Guantanamo Bay, is composed of ambient audio recordings and photographs, all vetted and edited by the United States Southern Command (US military).

Jordan was assigned two handlers, one to guide him around the camp and the other to guide the viewfinder of his camera, in some cases literally moving his shoulders so that what he captured was only what he was allowed to capture.[41]

Child: *What are they doing?*

Child: *They are blind and helping each other.*

So many verbal instructions. So many warnings.

And every evening Jordan's camera rolls and audio recordings were reviewed by Operational Security and deleted or cropped according to whatever taxonomies of permission Power preferred that day.[42]

In this sense, *Clearance Process* is an artistic collaboration with the US military, one in which Power contributed ideas on shot selection, composition and editing, as well as providing a curiously tuned filter for what sounds—such as the birds in Camp X-Ray, the now mostly overgrown and off-limits, original detainee camp—might clear Power's control.[43]

We cannot see pain in other people, only (sometimes) the effects of its presence. If we are sensitive, we might see pain redacted in people's skin and eyes, in their gait. Redacted but not erased.

Further, the relationships individuals have with pain differ from individual to individual. The relationships individuals have with different kinds of pain differ, too.

The English doctor from Cornwall held my hand in his hand and touched each knuckle. He moved my fingers, my wrists. To him, he said, everything felt right.

We can't measure pain but no one doubts it exists. What we doubt are the relationships people have with pain. We doubt the meaning of some pain, for some people, some of the time. We doubt the impact of pain.

We believe pain most fully when it appears as the symptom of something we can explain. Whether the explanation holds up under scrutiny or not.

Seven months after the walk—The Eyes-Closed Walking Tour, as Carmen has come to call it—I'll learn that one of the participants is a nine-year-old girl from Saskatchewan.

She's never visited this part of our city and will not return even though she spends the next two days touring the Okanagan with her family.

All she'll know of this delta of concrete is a slow, hour and a half, non-visual shuffle with her arm linked to the arm of a stranger,

a stranger who will later tell me about the girl in a restaurant at the edge of the cultural district, the windows of the establishment full of winter night and, outside, the sidewalks plaqued with ice.

"This blind man," Raymond Carver writes in the opening line of his story "Cathedral," "was on his way to spend the night. His wife had died."

The blind man's name is Robert, and his wife's name was Beulah. We learn this from the narrator's wife who, along with the narrator, goes unnamed, officially.

Robert calls the narrator "Bub," and the narrator calls Robert "the Blind Man." Bub calls his wife "my wife," and his wife asks if the narrator is "crazy" or "drunk."

Bub's wife worked for one summer in Seattle reading Robert "case studies, reports, that sort of thing."

For years after that, Bub's wife and Robert recorded cassette tapes that they sent each other via the United States Postal Service, telling of their lives—their feelings about their partners, the towns in which they found themselves mailing these tapes, about poems she'd written—

and in this way the two stayed in touch.[44]

There are different accounts.

According to one, the man from Burwash Landing enters my family story in the summer of 1977, the year before I was born.

In this account, my parents are driving north on the Cariboo Highway in a brand new F150 pickup with a man called Jimmy Donnelly.

I don't know much about Jimmy Donnelly except that he'd supposedly been arrested at the Maple Bay post office for importing LSD from England and served part of his sentence on a ranch near Quesnel, British Columbia.

Those things. And he always wore a cowboy hat.

"I felt like the world was a big huge black box that went on forever."

"I remember children loved us on this walk and said hilarious things like 'those people are learning to walk.'"

"Kind of like walking through a fog where things appear and disappear, based on motion and proximity."

"I felt I heard running water everywhere, as though it had always been there but had become background sound."

"Am I doing this right?"

"I just wanted to lie down on the grass outside the RCfo'thaA."[45]

"I liked it when we hit stairs and obstacles, but I also wanted to get some momentum in the open spaces."[46]

From this first, russet-coloured island in my meditation, I look for a second. Only water all the way to the horizon. Chromatic water. Chromatic sky. The lip of the horizon.

Then I turn around and remember the large island behind me, the one that was so obvious I'd forgotten it was an island. It stretches left and right to the edge of my vision. Lush green, dark, crowded with cedar trees.

Between the first island and the second, a series of barnacled rocks exposed at low tide. A land bridge. I plan to cross it when I remember that I've already built a bridge, one that floats above high water, made of wood and cables.

I cross the bridge I made.

He didn't recognize the F150, but he knew that hat belonged to Jimmy Donnelly.

And he knew the truck would stop not far up the highway at the roadside pub at Stony Creek. Because it was the 1970s and everyone stopped at a place called Stony Creek.

So the man from Burwash Landing walked back the way he came and into my story.

But "Cathedral" is not really about Bub's wife and Robert.

It's about how Bub, who is both afraid of "The Blind Man" and slightly jealous of him, realizes that Robert doesn't know what a cathedral looks like, doesn't know the difference between a cathedral and a "Baptist church, say."

Together, Robert and Bub draw a cathedral, first with Bub's eyes open, and then, after Bub's wife wakes up and opens her eyes

and sees the two
men drawing,

Robert's hand on her
husband's hand,

with Bub's eyes
closed, and without

cheating.

/

a   k

"How can we listen to redaction?" asks Jordan at the close of his introduction to *Clearance Process*. "How can we listen to whole systems of it?"

These are his animating questions entering a space in which the terms of engagement are almost wholly determined by Power.

And they have resonance for me with the questions that began to form around the Visual Inspection project: How can I make a work of art—poems, say—for someone whose body differs considerably from my own?

How can I listen to the pain of my body? How can I listen to the pain of others? How can I listen to whole systems of it?

Once a week all winter, I drop my daughter at school then wait in the parking lot in the plaza at Highway 33 and Hollywood for the pharmacy to open at 8:30 a.m.

The sky is washed-out grey, is the colour of my breath in the cold, is the pallor of the men in work boots and canvas dungarees waiting with me, silently, for their tiny paper cups of methadone.

Later in the clinic, I sit with a family of Syrians I see often when I come to get my shots: a mother, father, two boys and two girls, all under six. Through their interpreter I learn they were three years in a refugee camp in Greece. They're here today because they want more babies.

How to listen
for the encultured and genetic habits

of my body and mind? To gain clearance
to hear these aspects of myself?

To locate the influence of my embodiment
in my compositional choices? What do I do

with my body's hypersensitivity?
Its manifest pain? As in,

What have I already done?

Redaction is not the same
as absence. Rather

it is a matter of access. What are we
barred from? What is closed to us?

How does closure itself become
a site of pathos, something capable

of *moving* people? What redaction
is necessary? What would it mean

for the mind of the body
to give us access

to all the data it collects
over the whole of our corporeal lives?[47]

I want to ask these questions,
but I'm trying not to step on Taryn's heels.

b   r

e

    /   a

Before Carmen called it the Eyes-Closed Walking Tour, this experiment—a social practice art piece, really—was called Blind Field Shuttle.

If you google "Carmen Papalia Blind Field Shuttle" you can find videos of Carmen leading people with their eyes closed through New York City in 2014, San Francisco in 2012, Greensboro, North Carolina in 2016, and at Olin College in Needham, Massachusetts in October, 2015.

The Eyes-Closed Walking Tour invites participants to consider the emotional and pragmatic challenge of navigating built environments without sight.

The political dimensions of that challenge are multiple including the visual- and mobility-biased assumptions of urban design informed by the neoliberal economic dreams of Richard Florida and all the monorail salesmen of the world.

In 1987, while he lived in our basement with its dark wainscoting and low pile carpet, the man from Burwash Landing tested positive for human immunodeficiency virus (HIV).

I saw him once packing a box of condoms as he prepared to go on a multi-day hike with my dad.

His name was Rodney. He liked roses and compost and nettles.

There's also a video from 2015 of Carmen walking to the front lobby of the Albert and Victoria Museum in London. He is swinging his cane[48] widely across the sidewalk, hitting it loudly on walls and railings and parking meters.

In that video, one camera stares up at Carmen's face through something like a fish-eye lens as he makes his way down the street.

I wonder about my face as I listen to Carmen tapping with authority the sidewalks, hydrants, lampposts that we pass in our slow, multi-legged shamble.

As far as I know, Carmen has never seen the video with the shaky fish-eye frames of his face, nor any of the other videos Google can supply you with that feature him leading people through space.

He has never seen them because he can't see.[49]

One outcome of the tour might certainly be a summons to political activism, to a social engagement with Power that seeks to redress the inequities of our built environments and the basic social expectations of how people navigate those environments.[50]

For me, walking with my hands on Taryn's body, and Clay's hands on mine,[51] feeling my body tightening through the hour

and a half of awkward steps

—my neck, my back, my shoulders—

I am reminded of a line from Paul Celan: "Reality is not simply there, but must be fought for and won."[52]

"Sickness is the means by which an organism frees itself," wrote Rilke. "One must simply help it to be sick, to have its whole sickness and to break out with it."

Stevens' "Snow Man" and Robert Pack's commentary:

the anonymous mind that "becomes / one with the scene it
perceives, and at / that instant, the mind having ceased / to bring
something of itself to / the scene, the scene then ceases to exist //
fully."

The birds, the cars atremble as we cross in front of them, distinct
scent of lake water, canal water, deeply watered grass,

the gabble of children

and parents, oblivious, light through my eyelids, at first it alerts me
geographically, then slowly, less

████████

██████████

████████

The initial antiretroviral, AZT, went on the market in 1987, the same year a Canadian astronomer in the Chilean Andes reported the first supernova visible to the naked eye in nearly four hundred years.

Though it wasn't possible to see the exploding star from my position in the northern hemisphere, I have a false memory of witnessing the light through Rodney's spotting scope.

In 1987, on the Salish Sea, a positive diagnosis for HIV meant a redaction of certain imagined futures: Rodney would die. And he did, in 1995.

Reading from Hilton Als' *White Girls* to my daughter in 2015 when she was nine years old, the same age I was in 1987—when HIV is now, in Canada, a chronic illness and not a terminal illness—

it's almost as if history has been un-redacted.

"It was like nothing else in my life up to now," Bub says near the end of "Cathedral."

But it was like something in my life:

an adjustment. It was an adjustment, a lesson in how the body and mind begin to adapt, how perception begins to adapt.

Collaboration exists on a continuum—

or that's what one of my research assistants, Cristalle Smith, tells me over coffee while she's describing the zine she's making that allows readers to "choose your own adventure" with respect to kinds of collaboration.

At one end might be collusion and coercion—Vichy, France being the example *par excellence* of "collaborators" in this sense.

At the other end might be cooperation: people who elect to be in support of each other toward a goal.

That's one of Carmen's definitions of access:

"a perpetual negotiation of trust between those who elect to be in support of one another in a mutual exchange."

Somewhere in the grey middle might be co-dependency.[53]

What transpires in "Cathedral" is a collaboration that some days seems to epitomize the animating vision[54] of Visual Inspection.

At the behest of Robert, and with the wife watching, Bub closes his eyes and continues to draw the cathedral with Robert's hand on his. As Bub puts it, "[h]is fingers rode my fingers as my hand went over the paper."

And then in the penultimate paragraph Bub experiences the *jamais vu* of the Joycean epiphany: "I was in my house. I knew that. But I didn't feel like I was inside anything."

The predisposition of people like myself to certain allergic hypersensitivity reactions is called "atopy." From the Greek word for "placelessness," for the ineffable, the rare, the outstanding, the truly original experience.[55]

Atopy is said to have a high hereditary component: "Where am I?" babies cry as they enter the world. "Nowhere!" cries the enlightened nihilist with degrees from Johns Hopkins.

Maternal psychological trauma and prenatal programming are also considered strong progenitors for atopic syndrome.

Roland Barthes liked the word "atopy" with respect to texts and love. To have no subject, no theme is to be "atopic," without place.[56] To be yet unborn.

/ / / / k

One day I am talking to Dara—the Iranian-Canadian sculptor with
the blood disorder—and he's telling me about how he expects to
return to Tehran after his upcoming residency in Germany

because there are so many more opportunities for him there, how
oil money has made the conversion of factories into art spaces
possible, and how the prohibition on alcohol—and I don't entirely
follow this—means that many cafés also host large gallery spaces.

We're sitting outside a café on a half-sunny day in our small
Canadian city. While he's talking, I recall the ship of Theseus, how
human cells replace themselves.

Tina. Richard. Jonathon. Rodney exists. George exists. Mark.
And John. Ronald exists. Jorge. Steven. Charles. Carmen exists.
Jordan exists. Denise. And Erin. Karolina exists. Ashok exists. Ruth
exists. And David. Carol exists. Shelby exists. Lily exists. Erin.
Michael. ████████ exists. Katherine. Rodrigo. ████████████
Pat exists. Emily exists. Omar exists. And Rebecca. And Emma.
And Ollie. ████ Tomas exists. ████ Tanis exists. ████████
████████████ exists. And Taryn. Dara exists. And Matt. Clay
exists. Elaine exists. Neela exists. Robert. Wallace. Robert. Chris.
Saul. Robert. Lyle exists. And Elisa. And Nuala. And Cecily. And
Raymond. Robert exists. Beulah. Bub. And my wife. Thomas exists.
Paul. Brian. William. John. Hilton. Cristalle exists. Tyrone. Thom.
Karen. Michel. Tobin. Aubyn exists. And Cole. Peter exists. Helen.
Seamus. Simone. Melanie exists. And Jan. Nora exists.

My earliest memory: I'm standing at the railing of a crib. I see rows and rows of cribs, and a doorway. Beyond that, a hallway, maybe the edge of a desk.

Based on historical facts, I'm only four months old, alone at Royal Jubilee Hospital on Vancouver Island.

Or my memory comes from somewhere other than history.

My maternal grandmother said she could remember the ride home from the hospital in Winnipeg, near the end of the First World War.

In one guided meditation, I go back—before twelve, before seven, before three, before one, before the room of my birth, before I knew the word "atopy"—to the place my breathing first tightened.

I can't see anything—

On the second island, I find a small lake and swim in it.

Later, when a guide appears—someone from my past and present—I ask her to show me death. She takes me back to the small lake.

The insight of the body is that death is part of the body.

Then, from the dense temperate rainforest, steps a wolf I recognize as the grown version of one of the pups I'd seen on the beach with Rodney.

Who are you?

I'm curiosity.

—some pain
Is a dream but all true awakening a venom.

During the day, the stars are redacted by light.

Let's go back to a time before light, my friend suggests.

Before the door at the back of the eye.

I open my eyes, exhausted, in the courtyard where we began, the line separating now into its component parts, bodies drifting away in multiple directions, a few collapsing onto the small parcels of grass among the concrete.

Endnotes[58]

1   Alternate subtitles: *On His* ███████*; What We Talk About When We Talk* ███████; *Better Call Saul of Tarsus.*

2   Before it was a "project" in a formal sense, I mostly wanted to know how one of my visually impaired students could access small-press Canadian poetry books. A later pragmatic concern arose when trying to teach prosody: How to make the standard notations of slash and accent that illustrate metrical feet and patterns accessible? This student read with the assistance of a computer, but not only does a computer read without much awareness of vocalized stress patterns, it's incapable of incorporating these pedagogical marks. (To be fair, even a human reading these out loud would either have to describe the marks or grossly exaggerate the stress patterns.) Further, the line of poetry and the marks must be read together, simultaneously, in order for the lesson to be illustrated. Read in conjunction, the marks allow the line to be heard without exaggeration while still making relative stress patterns clear. The system is designed to assist people who have not developed a sensitive ear for this aspect of language—and there's no reason to believe that a visually impaired poet has developed such sensitivity. I'd be shocked to learn I was the first to articulate this problem, and not at all surprised to find that a solution or several already exist. Nevertheless, within the scope of our immediate resources it posed, and continues to pose, a fair problem. This sense of limitation, of scope, is central to the Visual Inspection project. While I did make queries about digital technologies—3D printers; interactive or responsive texts; the potentials of metadata and other digital humanities techniques, etc.—it was clear to me that, based on my own physical and health realities, engaging with computers and screens in this way would ultimately have the ironic effect of making the whole business less accessible to me. In other words, computers leave me feeling like shit, physically. The ethos of Visual Inspection has it that such limitations serve

as edges of meaning making, that they are to be respected, nurtured even, as sites of potential. Solutions to the problems described above may already exist for certain people in certain locations, but among the earliest insight of this project is that access is emergent, specific and perpetually negotiated. It wasn't simply a matter of not having enough resources to discover already existing solutions, but rather taking that ethos seriously and working within my limitations.

3   An infamously contentious realm that I've little to say about here other than to acknowledge the contentiousness. To paraphrase Jeff Jarvis, founder of *Entertainment Weekly*, disclosure is the new objectivity. In other words, to not acknowledge the contentiousness would be to ruin my credibility.

4   The eventual answer to my original research question is, in some ways, more straightforward: to make my poetry available to someone whose body works significantly differently than my own in a way that is consistent with my own preferences, I have to collaborate with that person. In other words, for me, this kind of availability is negotiated instance by instance. I have to ask, listen and respond, but, and this is where the way becomes less straight, I can't expect that each question, answer or response will be the same for every person, or even for the same person at every moment. One of the ways I approached the problem of prosodic notation described above was to hire a graduate student, Cole Mash, to make recordings that described the notation in context. This was done through consultation with the student who the recordings were meant for. I was reminded of this over coffee with Cole one morning two years later, near the end of drafting this manuscript. Cole was then working as a research assistant, helping me develop a bibliography, and (re)-imagining with me what might be made from the detritus the project had produced (literature matrices; conference proposals; grant applications; interviews

of the project team; and many drafts of different attempts to write about our findings). Cole's own research interests mirror Visual Inspection's: He's curious about how we might score on the page the para-linguistic dimensions of spoken poetic performance. Over coffee, he wanted to know why I didn't return to that original question at the end of the manuscript. I circle back to many other aspects, he told me, but the original question, he felt, was only ever addressed indirectly. The truth is that I'd come to regard the original question, and my answer, to be less compelling than the questions that had arisen subsequently. "A posteriori," as Cole put it that morning. I told him I'd write this note. As a record of one abandoned path and where it led.

5   Of course, dancers, actors, singers, performers of all kinds use their bodies as sites of composition, but writers tend to be more "thinky" as a friend of mine says, more detached. Scott and Papalia's work suggests to me ways in which the link between bodies and text might be made more present within literary composition.

6   And perhaps endless variations of Jordan himself? To what extent is our idea of Jordan, the idea that we might say *is* Jordan, emergent "within material intra-actions," as John Shotter says, "occurring in activities out in the world?" To what extent does the instrument play the musician, the game form the players, the language speak the speaker? How can we tell the dancer from the dance, as Yeats had it.

7   A typo in the first draft had it "later of façade," a near-pun I thought worth retaining here for the way it calls attention to the temporality of (false) surfaces.

8   From Karen Barad's "On Touching—The Inhuman That Therefore I Am."

9   Curious aspect of grammar: how the singular "pair" incorporates the multiple "doves."

10   In graduate school, the critic Karen Ford told me two
     important things that I've (mis)remembered frequently ever
     since. First, the longer you think on something the more it
     becomes clear that what you think and its opposite are true;
     therefore, what's worth saying is only what you still feel
     compelled to say when you've experienced this clarity. Second,
     ███████████ is only fully operative for a radius of about six feet
     around us.

11   A "fib" is a contemporary poetic form that builds itself via the
     Fibonacci sequence: In the case of *Alphabet*, the number of
     lines in each stanza grows accordingly. And, of course, lying.

12   člalqʷm̓, the docent explained, is a syilx game played with
     a set of small, specifically designed bones or sticks called
     skʼʷn̓kʼʷan̓t. One or more players holds the game pieces
     behind their backs and their opponent guesses in which hand
     the specific pieces are hidden. "Today, člalqʷm̓ is played by
     all ages," the docent later clarified via email, "as it helps us
     to learn the songs that go with the game as well as proper
     sportsmanship, but originally [it] was played by adults as a
     gambling game or as a way to negotiate as well as provide
     hospitality."

13   Where this book wonders how we might listen to whole
     systems of redaction and whole systems of pain, the
     pronunciation of nsyilxcən words requires a similar kind
     of listening to both the language as a whole system, and
     to the systems of being and knowing it arises from and is
     interconnected with. To listen to a word without its system
     of origin—or worse, to listen to it within the systems that
     have worked, historically, to erase and silence that word—is
     to risk assimilating that word into dominant, colonial culture.
     The connection between any language and its speakers is
     existential; in a colonial context, that connection is also deeply
     political. The inclusion of nsyilxcən words in this text arises

through consultation with, and guidance from, West Bank First Nation representatives, as well my own attraction to specificity and lexical diversity. It also poses some questions that rhyme with other concerns of the book regarding access. How do non-nsyilxcən-speaking readers of this book hear the nsyilxcən words? How then to gain access to these words and their pronunciations? Is such access important? Who is entitled to such access? According to the First People's Language Map of British Columbia, there are 359 fluent or semi-fluent nsyilxcən speakers and nearly 300 active learners.

14   Not poetry. Not poets. *Poetics.* "What is a poet for in a destitute time?" my friend will say over beers, mocking Heidegger. And me. Heidegger has one answer: to bring us into being. I don't think my friend cares particularly. Barad has sympathy for poets. Here she is on classical atomic models:

> Electromagnetic repulsion: negatively charged
> particles communicating at a distance push
> each other away. That is the tale physics usually
> tells about touching. Repulsion at the core of
> attraction. See how far that story gets you with
> lovers. No wonder the romantic poets had had
> enough.

15   Clayton McCann via email: "Paragraph 3, while enumerating the features of the 'arts district,' overlooks the microbrew tasting bar, a grievous oversight IMO."

16   For some years, a side element of my research involved "cultural mapping." In the week immediately following this walk, I participated in a symposium on Vancouver Island. From the program: "Where is Here? Small Cities, Deep Mapping and Sustainable Futures seizes on the tremendous interest shown in cultural mapping and placemaking practices by artists, researchers and small city placemakers, and brings to bear multiple knowledge-domains to move our collective

understanding of these practices forward." Before my presentation, I asked for the lights to be turned out.

17 Richard Florida, the progenitor and erstwhile proselytizer for the "creative cities" theory, which advocates the concentration of a "creative class" in urban centres as a driver of economic renewal, has a new book. Widely debunked in the last decade, Florida's theory is, nevertheless, sometimes credited for a revival in abandoned city cores like Pittsburgh, PA, and the "Anywhere, North America" style of development Carmen is leading us through art gallery by community theatre by regional library. The "gadabout urbanist," as Chris Selley calls him in the National Post, fears the results of his own advice and has set out on a tour to remedy his errors. Better call Saul of Tsaurus! Robert Oppenheimer! Anakin Skywalker! Recant, recant, recant! "When I listen to Florida talk," Selley writes, "I hear Lyle Lanley trying to sell Springfield a monorail."

18 All touching entails infinite alterity," writes Barad, "so that touching the Other is touching all Others, including the 'self,' and touching the 'self' entails touching the strangers within."

19 This word is mine, not Johnson's. I also toyed with "revealed," "uncovered" or even "unveiled" as words belonging to the lexicon of sight. "Sculpted" or "carved" also work if I want to emphasize the material manipulation of an existing text. I've left the verb "discovered" in the primary note—the first verb I deployed—because I am curious about the colonial reverberations that word has, particularly in a North American context. What could it mean to colonize an existing text, particularly one by a titan of English literature? Another verb with curious implications in this context: extract.

20 As of August, 2016.

21 From "The Rain Stick" by Seamus Heaney.

22   Taryn and I have never discussed the particulars of our
      pain in any medicalized way. While my conditions—largely
      immunological disorders of various presentations—have been
      pathologized (with numerous revisions) since I was three
      years of age, none of those diagnoses speak to the totality
      of my experience. Because these diagnoses offer insufficient
      terms of reference—they don't fully describe my symptoms,
      even within Western medical paradigms—and because pain
      experiences are famously mysterious and individual, speaking
      about it in medical terms often does more to undermine
      personal experience than illuminate it. Yet, those medical
      terms are, in most situations, the lingua franca of credibility.
      It's recognition within Western medicine that, for most people,
      allows understanding, accommodation and even feelings (like
      sympathy and compassion). We experience this even in our
      own bodies: doubt of our sensations until confirmed by lab
      work and magnetic resonance imaging. One thing—among
      many—that I am grateful to Taryn for is the belief, without
      questioning, of my experience as I reported it to her in
      conversation.

23   Not really blind, though that's the phrase—Justice is blind—
      but, temporarily blinded. Who tied the cloth over the eyes of
      Justice, anyway? What do they not want her to see?

24   The United States Southern Command spells this place name
      without an accent, while the Cubans include the accent.
      I've retained that small distinction in this text by using the
      anglicized format when referring to the detention camp and
      the Spanish-language format for the geographical place. I want
      to remember, with this detail, one of the ways the territory is
      contested.

25   A line of poetry is a *stich*, a word derived from Greek. Poetry
      composed with the line as the primary unit is called *stichic*. The
      slash used to indicate a line break when poetry is quoted in

prose is called a *virgule* and comes to us from Latin via mid-nineteenth-century French where it meant "comma." A *stanza* is a discrete set of lines in a poem, which Edward Hirsch calls the "natural unit of the lyric." In modern Italian a stanza is a room. In boxing a stanza is another word for a round of action. A professional boxing match can include up to twelve stanzas.

26　Jordan Scott discusses this research in *Lanterns at Guantánamo*. For further consideration see "Pauses in Deceptive Speech" by Benus, Enos, Hirschberg and Shriberg from the Department of Computer Science at Columbia Univerisity, SRI International in Menlo Park, and ICSI in Berkley, California.

27　The dead synecdoche: to "lose touch" with someone almost never means actual touch, but rather communication through the eyes and ears.

28　While drafting this document I solicited, via email, memories of this specific walking tour from participants. This account comes from one of those memories. The email responses served as another guiding of, as Clay put it, "the unlit day." These accounts interacted with my own memories in that peculiar way that (most) often happens with memories and imagination where the interpretive fictions of my own memory became indistinguishable, except through a few bare facts, from aspects of those accounts. The person who wrote about the line breaking in the middle of the road was closer to the middle of the line than I was, but I too remember the vulnerability of being paused in the middle of the road with cars waiting for us to cross.

29　Carmen asked us to close our eyes and say our names. This is a mostly accurate account of the names I heard spoken at the very beginning of the walk. Some people asked not to be photographed or identified as part of this event. In one case, a participant's mobility prohibited her from participating.

Carmen offered to design another kind of experience with her but that did not happen for reasons I'm not entirely clear about. This prohibition created important tensions that deserve to be mentioned. Taken as a political or "accessibility" tactic, the Walking Tour is open to some meaningful criticisms including its predication on certain normative assumptions about participants' mobility, as I outline below in these endnotes. However, Papalia is also working from within a particular philosophical framework (which I also discuss below). This framework, in my opinion, both addresses and embraces such tensions as sites of creativity.

30   I'm also tempted to say the tragic and the comic!

31   Is it possible that the US Military understands the "visual field" of poetry? Its difficulty? "Maybe they hired some MFA to explain it," Jordan speculates one morning over coffee and eggs. With poetry, you have to redact both what's there and what's not there. To have a mind of winter.

32   "The Snow Man" by Wallace Stevens. As Jordan says, it's only artists who preserve the white space "shagged with ice."

33   Also: alder. Birch. Cottonwood. Dogs. Cats exist. Feathers. Moulds. Ragweed. Chickweed. Sagebrush exist. NSAIDS. Peanuts exist. Oranges exist. Sesame. Wheat. Eggs exists. Eggs. Birch. Alder exists. Quinolones exist. Potatoes. Tomatoes. Eggs. Melons exist. Bananas. Penicillin exists. Cephalosporin exists. Beef. Corn exits. Corn. Eggs. Cats. Old World dust mites. Moulds exist. Wheat exists. Eggs. New World dust mites.

34   And who are these thinkers? I've lost track. But it sounds like something a childhood friend used to tell me when we were ten or eleven years old: everyone else is not real. "How do I know you're not made of bricks?" he would say. "Like inside, behind your skin: maybe it's just bricks." We lost touch but I've reasons to believe he makes rockets now.

35 A paraphrase from Robert Hass's "Meditation at Lagunitas," a poem I have paraphrased, quoted and misquoted, more than any other poem in my life.

36 How then does the façade of our perception redact our world? How do the instruments of our senses obscure via the convincing, yet largely inaccurate projections of the physical world they conjure for us in our minds? This is one of those moments where the epistemic and the ontological cannot be reconciled except through brutality.

37 Does it matter if we understand the science these phrases refer to? Does it need to be explained? For me they are as much metonyms for a particular epistemology we call medicine. And I like the rhyme "rate/migrate." Somewhere else they might be rhymed with "mitigate" and "infiltrate."

38 "In Kyoto..." By Bashō, translated by Jane Hirshfield.

39 *Paradise Lost*: Stanza 1 (1674 version) by John Milton.

40 My examples are deliberately "mainstream" or even "traditional," deliberately not "avant-garde" or "experimental." It's important to note that numerous practitioners of somatic-based poetics have grappled with the presence of the practitioner's body in the poem: as foregrounded in content, in form, in typography, etc... For a more extensive meditation on these practices I direct you to Thom Donovan's "part essay, part proposition, part thinking in motion" in *Jacket 2* called "Somatic poetics." For a brief primer on these issues, that also contextualizes some of Jordan Scott's work within "the return of affective modes of literary and cultural criticism in the last thirty years or so," I highly recommend Tyrone Williams "Aestheticizing the Stutter" on the Poetry Foundation blog, *Harriet*. In contrast, Visual Inspection proceeds from the assumption that the mind/body dualism is itself a construct and therefore all poetry is, in a very basic way, somatic. What interested me to begin with was not the possibility of an

analytical reading of somatic or embodied properties/dimensions/qualities in existing texts, but how the consideration of the poet's body in relationship to the body of a reader might influence synthetic, compositional practices. To put it another way, I was (am) less interested in what the reader can retrieve from the poem (per se) than, first, how and what the poet might use to compose the poem, and second, how the poet and reader might both participate fully in the work. While I don't address this directly here, this project has also engaged Indigenous, racialized, multilingual and gender nonconforming thinkers and artists with respect to the somatic or embodied aspects of their work(s)—work(s) that seriously, and importantly, challenges the conceits of my approach.

41 I am here resisting meditating, so obviously, on the word "capture." One aspect of Jordan's work that might deserve further consideration is the question of consent. For example, how to seek consent for recordings from incarcerated combatants? What kind of consent is possible in these circumstances? How to document the (perhaps) impossibility of consent? Another aspect is the racialized identity of the detainees. A third is translation of pain through first the interpreter's present during interrogations, and second in the English transcripts of Arabic responses.

42 "Blurring, smudging, fading, superimposing a black line or spot over certain parts of a photograph, or any other digital manipulation," writes Scott, "was not a substitution for cropping." Words then can be redacted, blacked out, covered over, but images themselves must be eliminated altogether. Words are symbolic to begin with and therefore, Power presumes, subject to effective erasure through symbolic gestures such as redaction, whereas a marked photograph draws attention to what is hidden (and in a digital age, the censoring mark might be decoded at a later date), thereby making it too dangerous to Power. But what of the extra-semantic value of

words? What about the way the black highlighting calls for their presence? There is pathos in the redaction of words, in the reminder that an act of communication is not simply absent, but just, somewhat arrogantly, obscured.

43   Or its stunted imagination. What Power "clears" is what it doesn't imagine returning as a force that might challenge it.

44   At the end of that summer working together, Bub's wife let Robert touch her face. According to Bub, Robert touched his fingers to "every part of her face, her nose—even her neck! She never forgot it. She even tried to write a poem about it. She was always trying to write a poem. She wrote a poem or two every year, usually after something really important had happened to her."

45   Rotary Centre for the Arts

46   Direct testimony from personal email correspondence: Michael V. Smith, Erin Scott, Taryn Goodwin, Clay McCann, Denise Kenney.

47   It would mean too much. It would mean an absolute cognitive/sensory overload. To a profound extent, our cognitive/sensory closure to aspects of our lives and world doesn't redact the world at all, but rather makes the aspects that we do apprehend apprehensible. Or put more simply, it makes the aspects. Full stop. Without that closure, without limits, the world doesn't really exist. Take the physicist turned popular writer, Brian Greene, proselytizer of string theory since 1999. The brutalism of his positivist take on physics has it that all aspects of existence are determined by nothing except the laws that govern the quantum particles that compose us. For example, "choice" for Greene is not really choice, but, at best, the feeling of choice. Setting aside the "truth" of this theory, in a human world that includes concepts of morality, value and free will, this line of thinking is, to my mind, paralyzing. It renders moot what we believe to be our most

operative tools of discernment. To borrow from Robert Hass, "talking this way, everything dissolves: *justice, pine, hair, woman, you* and *I*." If I could have an endnote to an endnote I'd add something about phenomenology.

48 Carmen had his cane stripped of its white paint to diminish it as a widely-recognized symbol of "blindness." The cane is now a dark graphite colour.

49 In our earliest conversations concerning "accessibility"—and my interest in making the visual dimensions of my work accessible to folks who can't see—Carmen described his ongoing frustration with photographic documentation of his work displayed in galleries, as well as his attempts to add dimensions, such as sound, that would increase his "access." For example, he once recorded the Walking Tour using multiple microphones at different points in the line. Later, Carmen told me that it was attending gallery openings with his friend, Aubyn, who would describe to Carmen not only the art, but the ducting in the ceiling, the red skirt of the woman making circular gestures with her hands as she talked, and the long shadows their figures made as they were captioned in the projector, that Carmen began to understand that it was the social dimension of art, the shared, collaborative experience, that most intrigued him.

50 Today on Facebook I saw a note describing "inaccessibility" as a "ban" on disabled people. Tobin Siebers, an influential scholar of disability and aesthetics, claimed that disability is the primary trope of contemporary social "disqualification." Meaning that tropes concerning the body of the Other give expression to the inferiority of certain identities: women as weak, black people as less intelligent, immigrants as sick, etc. There's a critique of the Walking Tour and other such social engagements that invite people to immerse themselves in particular disabilities (think of the Health and Exercise

Science students rolling around in wheelchairs for a day, as an example) that such activities belong to that same monorail salesman, neoliberal ideology that enacts such disqualifications: participants "experience" disability and thereby become morally ratified in their political activities— Let's sleep out on the street tonight to end homelessness! Let's shave our heads to cure cancer! Let's walk with our eyes closed so we can make sure every stoplight chirps at the proper pitch and decibel! But this moral ratification is bestowed by Power, and brings within the hegemony of Power even these purported exercises that John Dewey might've called "creative democracy." This is a fair critique since this kind of embodied social practice is neither new, nor necessarily accompanied by extensive theoretical framing. It's possible for Richard Florida to put his hands on your shoulders, close his eyes and be immersed in his own carnival-barker dreams. These are important areas of consideration, but they're not what I want to draw attention to here. I've always cared less for art as a tool of conversion than as a tool of exploration. If you feel you've explored the ground The Eyes-Closed Walking Tour explores, it's appropriate for you to move on. That doesn't diminish the potential of this experience for others to engage, or renew an engagement, with their own bodies in a social context.

51   I'm sensitive to the cultural synecdoche of "hands" in this context. Whiff of consumerism and patrolmen. Whiff of control. And here comes Foucault tapping me on the shoulder and whispering "panopticon."

52   A line Helen Vendler uses as an epigraph in the introduction to her typically convincing book on Seamus Heaney entitled *Seamus Heaney*. In "The Redress of Poetry," Heaney, quoting Wallace Stevens, describes poetry as the "imagination pressing back against the pressure of reality." For Heaney, poetry may not intervene directly in the political sphere but acts of imagination do add gravity, in the sense that Simone Weil uses

the term, to our lives, weight to the scales. Reality may need to be fought for but, in a Heaneyean conception, that fight emerges from imagined alternatives.

53 The Walking Tour is predicated on a series of what Papalia calls his "open access tenets" that exist in direct opposition to the concepts of universal accessibility and universal design. These tenets have been shared widely in talks across North America, the UK and Ireland, as well as through publication and personal communication. For Carmen, access is something that all people negotiate at all times regardless of embodiment. Because there is no normal body, the denial of access is contingent and specific, often socially determined. Therefore, Carmen rejects the idea that all possible iterations of access and denial of access could be foreseen (the animating vision of universal design). Further, Carmen proposes that such attempts to design something "accessible" to all people at all times is an expression of Power's hegemony, one that, under the guise of "accommodation," works to eradicate difference and individual autonomy. The "open-access tenets" resemble closely syndicalist political anarchism. Carmen's philosophy is radical in the sense of being from the root, where the root is the "participant's" body and "body of local knowledge." Respect for those roots combined with the self-elected participation in a supportive community lead to, in this post-disabled imaginary, "emergent, collectively held space in which members can find comfort in disclosing their needs and preferences with one another… a responsive support network that adapts as needs and available resources change."

54 It is an easy note to sound that descriptions of much activity are described in our language via the dead metaphors of vision, but it's a note worth sounding nonetheless.

55 The Greek word is ἀτοπία (atopia). From "a" meaning without, and "topos" meaning place. From my friend Mary Butterfield,

a Deweyan philosopher, via text: "Only your physical affliction would also have another meaning that relates to ineffability and experience."

56 Barthes uses the term in *A Lover's Discourse* to propose a register of language without predicate, something always changing. In a typically Barthesian way, the term is neither positive nor negative, but neutral. A kind of portal.

57 "Apitherapy" by Matt Rader.

58 At this point in my life, the best I can say about my thoughts, on any subject, is that I've had some. I've thought. I've recorded thoughts. This is an incomplete—and maybe unconsciously inaccurate—record of some of those thoughts.

Coda

One morning in August of 2017, I visited a radiation oncologist with my ex-wife Melanie to discuss the next stage of her treatments. That morning was the fifteenth anniversary of her mother's death from cancer. The coincidence invited meaning I resisted, though the chill I felt sitting in that air-conditioned hospital room reminded me that for many years after her mother's death, Melanie and I both felt August was a cool month with lousy weather.

The word "curious" comes from Latin via French and has as one part of its makeup the sense of meddlesome inquiry, of anxiousness. The last year of the Visual Inspection project included a number of curious coincidences. In the winter, my erstwhile research assistant, Clayton McCann, who did real yeoman's work on this project from the beginning, suffered a small stroke that left him struggling, at times, to find and form words when typing. In the spring, Jordan Scott suffered another concussion brought on by either a seizure or exhaustion. I had my own stint in the hospital with sepsis. Then in the week before the appointment with the radiation oncologist, the moon passed between the earth and the sun, an event I witnessed through a small panel of glass at a kangaroo farm in the central Okanagan. By far the most remarkable aspect of the eclipse was how quickly the air cooled without the sun.

In booksellers' catalogues, "curious" can also mean "erotic" or "pornographic." Though this is not a bookseller's catalogue, there *is* something curious in writing this way about bodies. Rodney died in 1995 of complications from AIDS. As a young person I remember thinking how unfair it was that this retro virus had turned Rodney's body into an open point of speculation for other people, that his dignity was impinged by the surveillance of our imaginations. Now, of course I know this is common for many racialized, sexualized and medicalized bodies. When Melanie was pregnant, women touched her belly without asking. Now people see her bald head and ask if she has a family history of breast cancer and if she nursed her babies. There's a figure standing naked behind this text: I write about ill bodies, disabled bodies, bodies in pain, not for titillation or pathos, but because these bodies are our own.

As you already know, this book responds to questions with more questions. Perhaps I took Chekhov too seriously when he said the role of the artist is to ask questions, not answer them. I knew early on that I would never arrive at a satisfactory answer to my original questions, that the work of this project hewed more to cultivating a kind of attention rather than solving a problem. The last time I spoke with Carmen Papalia he was wrapped in a blanket trying to find a way to talk about his own physical pain, to feel comfortable (if that makes any sense) with his pain as a subject. The young woman who set me thinking of all this was, for most of her life, barred by legal action from telling the story of her blindness. As I understand it, her limited vision was the result of medical negligence at a young age. The legal action was settled during the time she was my student, but she never disclosed any further details and I didn't ask. It was enough to know that she'd been prevented, by forces aligned with and against her interests, from telling that story. The pathos of her injury was sharpened by prohibition, absence, by redaction.

During the first days of a lunar cycle the moon is not visible except by the starlight the invisible moon displaces. This phase is called the new moon. I learned this from my father who owns an old wooden boat and sails on the Salish Sea, and therefore pays attention to stars and charts. He's also losing his eyesight due to scarring on his retinas. Because of the retinal damage, he sees small floating bodies in his vision. I imagine these as new moons: visible by what they obscure. He's also had a vitrectomy, the removal of the vitreous humor, the clear gel between the lens and the retina that is full of fibres and can further damage the retina as we age. "Vitreous" comes from the Latin for "glassy" and is a cognate of the term "woad," the common name of the flowering plant *Isatis tinctoria*, as well as the indigo dye that has been extracted from its leaves for millennia. In Dutch, my father's first language, the word is *wede*. My father's eyes are a much paler blue.

Melanie has blue eyes. During the writing of this text she underwent a partial mastectomy and sentinel lymph node dissection, six rounds of multi-chemical chemotherapy, and her first treatment of Herceptin, a targeted drug that blocks the HER2 receptor on the surface of the cancer cells, which in turn causes cells to die off. Soon she'll begin four weeks of daily radiation therapy, as well as the beginning of five to ten years of Tamoxifen treatment, which inhibits the estrogen production cancer cells need to grow. She's thirty-eight years old.

For a year before her diagnosis, I set about learning to identify the plants of the central Okanagan where we live. This was something I'd done in other places I'd lived as another way to cultivate a particular attention. One of the first plants I identified is called hound's-tongue for its rough, hairy, tongue-shaped leaves. Hound's-tongue, like *woad*, is considered a noxious weed, an invasive species, in this part of western North America. Why and how a plant takes hold in an ecosystem has in part to do with its genetics and in part the specific conditions of that ecosystem. What we do about that plant might more honestly take both these components into consideration. One Sunday in late spring, after Melanie's surgery and before her chemotherapy, after the flooding of 2017 and before the blooming of the hound's-tongue, we walked up a mountain near Kelowna some Dutch settlers called Spion Kop. From the top, we could see the deep indigo ingot of the lake, formed by and forming the valley.

Hound's-tongue is considered noxious in part because it can cause photosensitivity in animals that ingest it. My youngest daughter has an immunological condition that causes tiny, painless wheals to rise on her skin when exposed to sunlight. I sometimes can't see them until I run my fingers across the back of her hand. The doctors call this syndrome "polymorphic light eruptions." As if her skin were erupting in light.

September, 2017

BIBLIOGRAPHY

Alighieri, Dante, Sandow Birk, and Marcus Sanders. *Dante's Inferno*. San Francisco: Chronicle Books, 2004.

Als, Hilton. *White Girls*. San Francisco: McSweeney's, 2013.

Barad, Karen. "On Touching—The Inhuman That Therefore I Am." *Differences* 23, no. 3 (2012): 206–23.

Barthes, Roland. *A Lover's Discourse*, translated by Richard Howard. New York: Hill & Wang, 1980.

Bashō. "In Kyoto," translated by Jane Hirshfield. Accessed Dec 24, 2017. https://www.poetryfoundation.org/poems/48708/in-kyoto-.

Benus, Enos, Hirschberg and Shriberg, "Pauses in Deceptive Speech." *Speech Prosody*, no. 18 (2006): 2–5.

Carver, Raymond. *Cathedral*. New York: Vintage, 2015.

———. *What We Talk About When We Talk About Love*. New York: Vintage, 1989.

Chekhov, Anton P. *A Life in Letters*. London: Penguin Classics, 2004.

Christensen, Inger. *Alphabet*. Hexham: Bloodaxe Books, 2000.

Collis, Stephen and Jordan Scott. *Decomp*. Toronto: Coach House Books, 2013.

Dewey, John. *Art as Experience*. New York: Berkley Publishing Group, 1980.

Donovan, Thom. "Somatic Poetics." Accessed Dec, 24 2017. https://jacket2.org/article/somatic-poetics.

Dont Look Back. Directed by D. A. Pennebaker, et al. New York: The Criterion Collection, 2015.

Florida, Richard. *Cities and the Creative Class*. London: Routledge, 2005.

Foucault, Michel. *Discipline and Punish: The Birth of the Prison*. New York: Knopf Doubleday Publishing Group, 1995.

Glück, Louise. *Wild Iris*. New York: Harper Collins, 1993.

Hass, Robert. "Meditation at Lagunitas." Accessed Dec, 24 2017. https://www.poetryfoundation.org/poems/47553/meditation-at-lagunitas.

Heaney, Seamus. *The Redress of Poetry*. New York: Farrar, Straus and Giroux, 1996.

————. *The Spirit Level: Poems*. London: Faber & Faber, 1996.

Hirsch, Edward. *A Poet's Glossary*. Boston: Houghton Mifflin Harcourt, 2014.

Homer, and Angus M. Bowie. *Odyssey*. Cambridge: Cambridge University Press, 2013.

Johnson, Ronald. *The American Table: More than 400 Recipes that make Accessible for the First Time the Full Richness of American Regional Cooking*. New York: Pocket, 1986.

————. *Radi os*. Albany: Sand Dollar, 1977.

Lakoff, George, and Mark Johnson. *Philosophy in the Flesh: The Embodied Mind and its Challenge to Western Thought*. New York: Basic Books, 1999.

Milton, John. *Paradise Lost*. London: Pearson Education, 2007.

————. *The Poetical Works of John Milton*. London: J. and R. Tonson in the Strand, 1761.

The New English Bible: New Testament. Oxford: Oxford University Press, 1961.

Onbeing.org. "Reimagining the Cosmos." Accessed 24, Dec 2017. https://onbeing. org/programs/brian-greene-reimagining-the-cosmos/.

Pack, Robert. *Belief and Uncertainty in the Poetry of Robert Frost*. Lebanon: University Press of New England, 2003.

Pappalia, Carmen. "An Accessibility Manifesto for the Arts." Accessed Dec 24, 2017. https://canadianart.ca/essays/access-revived/.

————. "The Blind Field Shuttle Walking Tour." Accessed Dec 24, 2017. https:// vimeo.com/78862660.

Pinsky, Robert. *The Sounds of Poetry*. New York: Farrar, Straus and Giroux, 1999.

Plutarch, et al. *Plutarch: Lives that made Greek History*. Indianapolis: Hackett Publishing Company, 2012.

Rilke, Rainer M. *Letters to a Young Poet*. London: Penguin Random House, 2011.

Scarry, Elaine. *The Body in Pain: The Making and Unmaking of the World*. Oxford: Oxford University Press, 1985.

Scott, Jordan. *Clearance Process*. Vancouver: Small Caps Press, 2017.

————. *Lanterns at Guantánamo*. Burnaby: Simon Fraser University Department of English, 2007.

Selley, Chris. "Sorry, Richard Florida, but Kathleen Wynne Is No Urbanist Saviour." Accessed Dec 24, 2017. http://nationalpost.com/news/toronto/ chris-selley-sorry-richard-florida-but-kathleen-wynne-is-no-urbanist-saviour.

Shape Arts. "Getting to the Front Lobby." Accessed Dec 24, 2017. https://www. youtube.com/watch?v=DuCbUeqhBEQ.

Shotter, John. "Agential Realism, Social Constructionism, and Our Living Relations to Our Surroundings: Sensing Similarities rather than Seeing Patterns." *Theory & Psychology* 24, no. 3 (2014): 305–25.

The Simpsons. "Marge vs. the Monorail." Directed by Rich Moore. Twentieth Century Fox, 1994.

Stevens, Wallace. *Anecdote of the Jar.* Amherst: Prometheus Press, 1982.

Techcrunch.com. "Jeff Jarvis: When it Comes to New Journalism, 'Transparency is the New Objectivity'." Accessed Dec 24, 2017. https://techcrunch. com/2011/05/23/jeff-jarvis-when-it-comes-to-new-journalism-transparency- is-the-new-objectivity/.

Tyrone Williams. "Aestheticizing the Stutter." Accessed Dec 24, 2017. https:// www.poetryfoundation.org/harriet/2017/04/aestheticizing-the-stutter.

Vendler, Helen H. *Seamus Heaney.* Cambridge: Harvard University Press, 2000.

Virgil, John Dryden and Frederick M. Keener. *Virgil's Aeneid.* London: Penguin Books, 1997.

Weil, Simone, et al. *Gravity and Grace.* Winnipeg: Bison Books, 1997.

Wikipedia. "Rendition." Accessed Dec 24, 2017. https://en.wikipedia.org/wiki/ Rendition_(law).

Zach Bergman. "Carmen Papalia: Blind Field Shuttle." *C : International Contemporary Art* 121 (2014): 43.

ACKNOWLEDGEMENTS

The Visual Inspection research project was financially supported by the Hampton Fund for Emerging Scholars, The British Columbia Arts Council, The Faculty of Creative and Critical Studies and the University of British Columbia's Work Study program. Special thanks to the research assistants who worked on this project: Clayton McCann, Cole Mash, Juawana Grant and Cristalle Smith.

A deep gratitude to my collaborators, Carmen Papalia and Jordan Scott. Their guidance on all matters Visual Inspection (and *Visual Inspection*) was essential. Thank you also to Taryn Goodwin and Erin Scott who contributed their invaluable presences at critical times. Thank you to museum assistant Coralee Miller, and cultural administrator Jordan Coble at the Sncəwips Heritage Museum for their gracious and generous teachings.

The Visual Inspection project, quite simply, would not have happened without Dr. Mary Butterfield, first in the Office of Research Services at UBC, and later in the Faculty of Management.

Thank you to Amber McMillan, Silas White and Carleton Wilson at Nightwood Editions for helping me create this book.

Visual Inspection exists through a community who elected to be in support of each other. That community contributed their stories, bodies and songs.